Light Is Life

Henry Langhorne

Pelican Press Pensacola
Pensacola

Light Is Life
Copyright © 2017 by Henry Langhorne

ISBN   978-0-9911640-7-3

Pelican Press Pensacola
PO Box 15131
Pensacola, FL 32514-0131

www.pelicanpresspensacola.com

Cover photo credit to J. D. Hayward Photography

To those who have lived a long time and lost many friends, especially those who have seen the darkness of night approach them yet fade in the brightness of light.

TABLE OF CONTENTS

TABLE OF CONTENTS....continued

PREFACE

Light is essential for life. Fourteen billion years ago did light not bring life to our new universe in a cosmic explosion? Imagine life without light.

A near-death experience made me even more aware of my own mortality and the significance of light in our lives. It is ironic that I, a cardiologist, was blind-sided by a cardiovascular disorder. I survived because of excellent medical care. This experience allowed me to see the light of life in new ways: light overwhelming darkness, light pouring into matter, even light shining on water's skin or filtering through the branches of winter-sleeping trees.

The Bible acknowledges the role of light in these quotes from the Book of John:

In Him was life; and the life was the light of men. John: 1: 4

I am the light of the world: he that followeth me shall not walk in darkness, but shall have the light of life. John 8: 12

Light Is Life is composed of four sections. The first includes poems written as soon as I recovered from the near-death event. The second consists of poems written during Lent of 2016—when I decided to stop giving up peach ice cream and write some Lenten poems instead. I call them my "Preacher Poems." The third section is a selection of previously published poems, and some of these "Old Favorites" have been revised to more closely fit the theme of this volume. The last section consists of new poems.

There is so much I owe in gratitude to all the faculty of the School of Letters directed by John Grammer at The University of the South. This faculty guided me on a course of learning in poetry and fiction that enabled me to obtain my MFA (Masters of Fine Arts) in Creative Writing in 2016. My advisors, Daniel Anderson and Charles Martin, were of invaluable help during that time and in my thesis preparation.

I am also grateful for the continued support of the West Florida Literary Federation, especially Andrea Walker. My editor, Linda Wasserman, has again displayed her talents in reviewing my work for grammatical errors, offering helpful suggestions, and also supervising publication by Pelican Press. The expertise of Jimmy Hayward again has provided the excellent photography on the book's cover as on my previous publications.

Henry Langhorne
March 2017

Near-Death Poems

Lighten our darkness, we beseech Thee, O Lord, and by thy great mercy defend us from perils and dangers of the night.

The Book of Common Prayer
Evening Prayer Service

Respite

On my eighty-fourth birthday
I did not know
I had a rendezvous with death.

Fifty years of doctoring
had taught me
most had some kind of warning.

It was sudden and painless
as it overwhelmed me
and put my mind to sleep

as it did before I was born.
But then I awoke
and thanked everyone.

Last Words

Is it hubris to think
the sky may darken
if it's daylight, or brighten
if it's nighttime,
when I die?
More likely, it will
do nothing at all.

What may stop things,
for a moment,
will be the words I find
for the last bit of light
I will see. Those words
must be memorable.

Revised from original in
The Lay of the Land

Empty Chair

When families lose a venerable one
they may preserve a seat at the table

for that departed person
when celebrating birthdays and holidays.

At first they acknowledge the absence
with their favorite memories,

children and grandchildren especially,
to support a grieving spouse.

Yet history closes up quickly
around the table as time moves on.

The lost one is missed mightily,
but they all go on with their lives

until a day when no one at the table
pauses to stare at the empty chair.

August 1, 2016

The Soul's Sigh

What is the sound of faith

that the near-dying long to hear

when restrained in a bed in CCU

and hooked to a breathing machine?

It is the soul's sigh as we breathe

together the invisible gift of air.

Everyone needs it—

every living organ—

even the soul who makes

this earth an island home.

Before I Die

I need to clean up
the stains of years

that remind me
how indifferent lives

drift by us like water
and leave us

with broken dreams
and tearful memories,

even discolored
and crooked toenails.

Before I die
I need good dreams

again—and friends.
I need a pedicure.

To the Nurses of CCU

I now return to the place I survived

because of your many skills.

When I think of all you did

to bring me back, my heart fills

with such gratitude I tell my tale—

each of you Florence Nightingale.

Christmas Eve
2016

Dead Battery

A month of critical care in a hospital
was dealt to me as my summer vacation.
Thanks to electricity skillfully applied
to my heart, I came home again.

Everything was working: lawn sprinklers,
security system, air-conditioning—
as if I had never been away.
Life clearly had gone on without me.

My first effort to venture out again
was a trip to see my doctor,
but my trusty Jaguar, only twelve years old,
was dead silent when I turned the key.

The AAA man was prompt in his truck.
With clean jeans and T shirt, face perspiring,
his honest eyes told me I was in luck.
He worked diligently with cables and wires
to revive the dead battery but failed.

Unlike my case, electricity did not bring it life,
so he replaced the battery with a new one.
After his version of a heart transplant,
he smiled and told me to have a blessed day.
He said my old Jaguar, alive again, was beautiful.

August 21, 2016

My Discharge Summary

After two weeks of critical care,
I sensed improvement enough
to begin planning my own discharge.
The tubes had been removed—
except for the one in my bladder.

Though still lost in time and place
I could swallow when fed
and walk in the hall with an escort
who pulled my IV pole with its bottles
of nutrient fluids and urine.
Even using a walker I staggered,
my untied gown gaping open,
my backside on display.

The days and nights were as jumbled
as my mind, but as I dozed one day,
I decided it was time to go home
and open my bed for someone sicker.
This required a discharge summary,
so as I lay dozing—always dozing—
I dictated my hospital stay in detail
to my daughter as she sat beside me:

the course of my illness, test results,
drugs used. I even interpreted
my own EKG. My diet and medications,
activities and return visit were all included.
Only then did I drift into contented sleep.

Baptist Hospital
June 2016

Light Is Life

It was sudden—my collapse.
Heart and kidney abruptly on strike
after eighty-odd years of service.
My new home, a coronary care unit,
all lights and shrill alarms, no windows.

Comatose, I was spared the noises
and unforgettable smells, the insult
of tubes seeking to invade every orifice—
my arms and legs bound in restraints,
my skin a bruise of endless needle sticks.

Still unconscious and on a respirator
with a tube down my throat
I dreamed (I guess it was a dream)
I was in my childhood Sunday School room,
my family sitting ahead of me.

It was dark in the room but I could see them.
Each one urged me not to give up,
not to lose sight of the light.
Outside the school window were the graves
of my father and my grandparents.

I kept looking out of the window,
searching for some light in the darkness.
Then I saw a building, all dark
except for a steel pipe running down its side.
A beam of light reflected off the pipe.

This light spread across the graveyard
and into my Sunday School room.
There it overwhelmed the darkness
around me and poured itself into my life.
I would not yet go into that night.

Preacher Poems

God goes, belonging to every riven thing he's made
sing his being simply by being
the thing it is:
stone and tree and sky,
man who sees and sings and wonders why

— Christian Wiman
Every Riven Thing

Ease My Loneliness

Lord, how is it now

my childhood should rise

again to haunt my mind?

Suffer that child who lived

on sunlight and the solitude

of a silent countryside.

Help me now to bear

old wounds of body and spirit

for which I still care.

Ease my loneliness—

embrace the child again.

Lent 2016

In Dream One Winter Night

In dream one winter night
I disinterred the grief of living,

the night bird's wailing call,
freezing rain and wind in my face,

and sad breeze-shaped clouds
returning from a godless place.

Then, I felt life crawl through me,
an incarnate thought as if

it came, perhaps, from God,
beyond all idea of beyond.

Lent 2016

When Life Dies

Did Light bring Life to our new universe
around fourteen billion years ago
in a cosmic explosion?

We are told that light has been essential
 to life in all forms that have evolved
since light elements were born.

Even when Life dies there still is Light
shining somewhere in the room
or in the windows to the world outside.

For the dead the people pray—
Give to the departed eternal rest;
Let light perpetual shine upon them.

The Prayers of the People, Form III
Book of Common Prayer

House in the Woods

A long-abandoned house

only someone lost could find,

with paneless windows and open doors

seems both a ghost of the life

that once happened here

and a living spirit of this wasted place.

Give it breath, Lord. Give it grace.

Lent 2016

A Gift After Golgotha

He endured it all,
even the vinegar sponge.

Those standing below,
His mother Mary,

Mary Magdalene,
John, the disciple He loved,

all suffered too.
On the third day—

if we could give them a gift—
the Hallelujah Chorus

from Handel's Messiah.
Unlock them with music.

Good Friday
March 2016

The Search Endless

The search endless

to find Him

church, synagogue, mosque

all empty of evidence

Then the wind

proclaims

He is existence

February 29, 2016
Lent

In the Garden of His Grief

Fear of change, of failure, of dying
grows in him because he holds
himself willfully apart from God.

He tries refusing to acknowledge
his fear by dulling this worry
with alcohol or entertainment

or long despairing walks.
Perhaps he can find the strength
for a furious resistance and achieve

success, but then a shell might grow
around the soul God is trying to refine.
He could turn to dust inside that shell.

But if he ventures close to Christ
and gives up his failing struggle,
they could build a home together.

The two could fashion dovetail joints
made of imagination and experience,
and they could clear his garden of grief.

Lent 2016

To Depart in Peace

How do we depart in peace?
your servant asks,

his body racked with pain.
How have our eyes seen

the glory of Your salvation?
It comes with pain, doesn't it?

Pain that brings faith
from every corner of the room,

pain and faith so married together
they see the glory of Thy salvation.

Lent
February 29, 2016

A Chinaberry Tree and Me

A storm in my boyhood almost blew it
out of the backyard.
There seemed no reason
the chinaberry tree was singled out
from all the other trees.

As a boy, I thought its closeness
to my bedroom window must have given
it the chance to survive
as it bent almost to the ground.
Perhaps its roots were just stronger.

For nights and years on end
I watched the tree endure the wind.
Then we became survivors together
when the storm singled me out one night
but spared me as it did the tree.

It seemed there was something
at the heart of things that had willed it so,
something I will have to cling to
when, one night, the storm
finally returns for us—as I know it will.

Voices

Someone, without knowing it,
can say goodbye forever
with a voice that vanishes in the fog.

After we put on winter clothes
more and more voices are heard
that tell us we will die—

If we lie down under winter stars
the cold will begin to fill our bodies
when night comes on.

Instead we should listen to voices
that tell us to stand and serve Him
with gladness and singleness of heart.

The Book of Common Prayer
The Episcopal Church

24

Survival

No one gets by
without suffering.
Surviving is personal,
but awareness of decay
of the body
makes it easier,
some say.

Survival's abiding presence
allows suffering
to bring sorrow
and loneliness
to the soul.
Yet, thanks for the day,
some say.

Lent 2016

There Is a Time

Last night's stars are west; those above us,
dead a million years, are only stardust.

Tired of the promise of resurrection
and holding things mortal with affection,

like a child with a favorite toy, we know
we must choose a time to linger, to let go.

Our lives become photographs yellowing
in someone else's scrapbook as we know

it's time to balance books with those who care,
time to leave nothing in the house but prayer.

There is a time to die
and we will all see it in...
— John Donne

The Sycamore Tree

For ages some of us have looked in vain
for a chance to be seen and repent.
One recalled what he learned in Sunday School—
a story about a rich tax collector
named Zacchaeus who wanted to be changed
by Jesus who was passing through Jericho.
Short in stature, Zacchaeus could not see
above the crowd so he climbed a tree—

not any old tree but a sycamore.
Jesus saw him, called him down,
and announced he would stay at his house.
Zacchaeus promised to give to the poor
and repay anyone he had defrauded.
Thus salvation came to his house.
Those who heard and believed the story,
have tried many ways to seek repentance.

Finally, one believer found an old church
surrounded by a wall he could not see over.
He climbed a sycamore tree, no less, and watched
the poor, the destitute, file into the church.
Then he came down and walked inside
to empty his wallet in the collection plate.
Such blessings happened over and over
once the sycamore tree was found again.

— Luke 19:1-10

New Lenses

Those of little faith
are often told to look for signs,
to be alert, to question.
and above all, keep trying.
Today the sky was empty

of clouds until
a single white cumulus
suddenly appeared,
followed by a parade
of sizes and shapes

I have never seen before.
Later, as I looked up
at trees in my backyard,
their branches appeared alive
in their wind-stirred motion.

Not in a lifetime of looking
at clouds and trees
have I seen them so,
or do I see them
through a new pair of lenses?

March 6, 2016
Lent

Old Favorites

A good poem helps to change the shape of the universe, help to extend everyone's knowledge of himself and the world around him.

— Dylan Thomas

Poetry writing is more humane than life. It is full of second chances. Your sentence, so to speak, can always be revised. You can fix the inappropriate, adjust every carelessness, improve what you felt.

— Stephen Dunn

Funeral Friends

When I die I will step through the door
in awe of what it will be like inside
that cottage of darkness.

There, I will seek the light
until there is light in every room
and, with it, the life of all who enter.

At my memorial service, I will sit
in the back pew and smile
at the eulogies, the favorite hymns

they sing as they grieve in stanzas.
It will be fun to see old friends
shuffle into pews and endure

reading the burial service
they almost know by memory.
I would like to tell them I tried

to hold my world in my arms,
but now that it's over, it doesn't matter
if my struggle failed or not.

It was a trip to remember.

Revised from original "When I Die" in
The Lay of the Land

After Bypass Surgery

I awake alone,
the light dim in my cubicle—
the uninvited guest
who had squeezed my heart
with his big, hot hands,
now gone.

I lie in a bubble of air
so pure I think of prayer
and distant saints of childhood.
A nurse's mother-face wavers
before my eyes
as she changes my soaked gown.

I listen to the *whish thump*
of an oxygen machine cycling,
and a clock's exaggerated tick.
A net of IV tubes that trembles
like tinsel and twisting silver
feeds me—pain's fire doused
by needle stick.

Published JAMA
July 5, 2016

Presto Passion

legs spread she embraced

his brown body between her knees

his neck raked back

on her shoulder of emerald sequins

her green satin skirt pulled back

while an adagio of movements

pervaded the room

her left hand stroked his neck

the right caressed his back

with gentle then faster strokes

to allegro to presto

until climax won applause

Pensacola Symphony
Fall 1991

Aftershave

Ruby was a flirt at eighty
blue-tinted hair in place
rouged cheeks and dentures
her look said she knew men

She went to Europe last fall
and brought me a present
expensive Armani cologne
I saved for special events

At dances and cocktail parties
I wore her smell
They found her dead
beside a picture frame

of Ruby and Abe cutting cake
in the Bronx vintage 1930
Tonight I wake up
and smell Ruby beside me

Spirits

Dust to dust, what comes
between is what we call living.
Do we stay the same dust
or change to something else,
the way a lie may pass
from mouth to mouth
and change into the truth?

As children we were taught
to look up to the sky
when we thought of spirits.
Not seen, perhaps they hid
and beat their wings
like angels in the trees.

Those of us who have seen
nothing in the clouds
may have missed them.
Perhaps we should look
below ferns and flowers,
under rocks and cedar beds.

One evening a moth rapped
with its dusty knuckles
against the window pane,
turning white, then silver,
a moment you could almost
be certain you had a soul.

Mama

they said she asked for me
so I am here again
in her dining room
where we once were all together
at the moment
she does not know me
there are only empty chairs
and pictures on the wall

she fixes me broiled chicken
and rice
and frozen vegetables
in little bowls
like children's trays
on holidays
I came to see her again
and watch her thick white hair
swirl in the kitchen.

The Empress Was Ice Cream

To Wallace Stevens
(1879—1955)

I was a soda jerk at Rexall Drugs
every Saturday from eight to eight
with Shirley, an auburn-haired cheerleader
boasting freckles and a pair of great legs
I could not appreciate back then.
Twelve year old boys thought about air rifles
and rubber gun wars Fridays after school.
They played marbles with a favorite aggie
and worried about Zorro and Tom Mix.

Shirley's steady came in early evening,
before the Hit Parade blared from an old
Philco radio on the back counter.
She made him chocolate malts (and never charged)
while they listened to the top ten songs
of the week, in rapt anticipation.
My thrill was the ice cream in cylinders
beneath the counter, waiting for me
to dip down, deep into the cold darkness
of luscious tastes and dependable pleasure,
always there for the taking,
the best of all Saturday night dates.

One night he did not come to see Shirley,
and as I dipped a cone of chocolate chip,
she slid behind me, brushing my back side
with firm thighs, and smiling when I quivered
so slightly, as when one swallows too much
cold ice cream. Instead of turning around,
I flipped open the first vat before me,
and while Sinatra crooned her favorite tune,
I spooned out a mouthful of soft fresh peach,
swallowing it with one passionate gulp.

Uniontown, circa 1944

37

Philco Wings

I put her
in a congregate nursing facility
where she clings
to her morocco scrapbooks
and fumbles with remote TV
from her chair
across this gulf.

Does she miss her old set
the knobs that turned life
off and on
the radio by her bed
on New Year's Eve
flying her on Philco wings
to Times Square?

Northpointe Retirement Home
1990

Tub Bath

we used to bathe together
father and son
I sat in front
and sailed plastic boats
in a warm sea
bound by his legs
strong as walls
that kept the waves calm

tonight there is no one
to scrub my neck
and guard the foamy bay
the sea is empty
of sailing ships
and cold waves beat
against my back

Father's Day
June 19, 1970

Thanksgiving on Omaha Beach

The day, a long walk together
on the wet beaches—
here and there a memory
of broken bodies rearranged
in the symmetry of white crosses—
ground lapis for the sky
where only swallows dogfight—
behind thick hedgerows
a church spire aimed at the dome
of a chilling Norman day.

They had waited beyond the red tide,
like brides, to surrender
limbs or lives—those heroes
generals love to worship.
Late in the wind-worn afternoon,
before the unplowable prairie of night,
it came—just at sunset—
the sudden pathos of soft rain.

Normandy
November 1999

40

Was It Really Poetry?

What do you do when the words
don't come to you anymore
and you no longer hear a dove
in the cedars at first dark?

When stars have become silent lights
drifting out of sight
and you live at the end of a road
where darkness begins?

Perhaps you thought
you were speaking your words
to men and women who listened.
Perhaps you imagined

they were your words only—
the children you gave birth to
in your restless dreams.
Or was it a universal voice

speaking to no one in particular,
that is, no one at all?

Good poets know their job is not to offer the truth,
but to be persuasive about their version of it.
— Stephen Dunn

Young Woman in a Red Coat

It was a cold Sunday morning.
The pews filled slowly
with its penitents bound
in heavy coats, all in stages
of aging. She walked past,
her red coat and scarf
adding freshness to the scene.
She sat in front and smoothed
her rich brown hair.

I did not see her face.
When she walked alone
up the steps to the chancel
and kneeled for communion,
her stride was confident.
How many years of grace
would she enjoy before wrinkles,
gray streaks, and painful hips?
Best I never saw her face.

*Poetry is the imagination pressing back against the
pressure of reality.*
— Seamus Heaney

The Forties

They were glorious years for the most part,
the challenge a war we fought as boys
crouched in foxholes with Daisy air rifles,
firecracker grenades, and Sterno stoves
Every back yard boasted a victory garden.
We saved paper and scrap metal
and wore aircraft spotters' blue armbands.

Of course there were sad moments
when Ennis Washburn, my boyhood idol,
was shot down over Guadalcanal,
and Jack Tate lost an arm on Iwo Jima.
We drove in cars with gas ration stickers
in the corner of the windshield
and saved allowances to buy war bonds.

We would survive Normandy and Bastogne
and later bask in the glory of our salad days.
It was the forties—the quintessential decade—
when we rocked on front porches
watching lightning bugs on summer nights
flitter together with their warm secrets
with nothing to worry or wonder about
except where they slept during the day.

Sunday Church

Going to church today
is not as easy as walking
a gravel road to Uniontown
past Cottonwood Creek
and cotton fields
while the sun shone hot
and mules stood in shade.

Churches were filled
before bells rang in the tower
men perspired
in dark vested suits
women in hats and veils
stirred the still air
with funeral parlor fans.

There was no organ music
the congregation sang
their favorite hymns
and sermons set
the shields of war on fire.
Before the communion rail
my knees ached on cool brick.

Uniontown
circa 1945

The secret life of poetry is always paying homage to the past, extending a tradition into the present.
— *Mark Strand*

44

To a Confessional Poet

You remind the room
that your mentor believed

one should write about
what others tell us to forget.

You startle us
with an open diary of pain

and profanity unlike
the sacrament of penance.

We are priests
attentive to your words

and yet we wonder
if your scars run deeper

than those borne
by others in this room.

Perhaps their silence
speaks for everyone here

who listens to your poem
without a tear.

It's fine to reminisce
but no one cares

about your childhood—
perhaps not even you.

Poetry Workshop, Key West
February 2000

Ballerina

My blue heron

looks back one million years

from the muddy bank

and is ready for lift off

it dips and rises

through a shower curtain

of dragonflies and pollen

it wants to be alone

to stand on one leg forever

to be a ballerina

Reparation for My Hometown

Churches have been falling down
since Shiloh and the Ark.
In my church the roof still leaks—
long after the children moved away
for jobs in the city.
Molding leaves cover names
on family graves.
Only the old remain
to defend our town.
They go to bed unarmed
to face the terror of night.

Build them a cathedral
in the square with rose windows
and flying buttresses.
Crown each new mayor.
Marry the young in the long nave
under stained glass windows.
Bury the dead with a requiem
meant for an emperor.
Let gargoyles guard the towers
and shriek at the night.

My Lady's Slipper

For my wife

Your father planted his seed well
that cold November night
You blossomed in your greenhouse
into the perfect lady's slipper
the envy of every orchid

Your petals were cheeks in blush
one soft and lip-shaped
your nectary filled
with the drink of the gods

I the bee you chose
to lie down beside you
from the swarms attracted
by your beauty

In spring when pollen makes
new life you taught me
the tender gestures one learns
in a lifetime of love

Now as winter stands outside
I lie beside you in our greenhouse
infatuated with your loveliness
enchanted by your grace

To Lose Everything

In the chill predawn fog
of a final wish in the world
someone loved dies,
and someone's life is changed,
but then, at what moment
of all our moments
is life not utterly changed,
until the final, most momentous
change of all?

In the mirror what we see
reminds us we won't be here
forever—that to grow old
is to lose everything.

Even when we are young
we glimpse it briefly
when a grandparent dies.
In time pets and parents
die, the unfortunate lose
a child, old friends estrange
themselves, a spouse is taken.
Yet in the midst of sorrow
we find joy in the living cosmos,
in its gloom, its terrible beauty.

When our souls are ready
we should affirm it is fitting
and proper as we grow old
to lose everything.

Thanksgiving at Morrison's

They huddle together like quail
flocked before a baited field
waiting for the door to open
grandmothers, great-grandmothers
clutching pocketbooks
to their forgotten breasts
stumbling inside
shuffling in line
the nodding gray heads
speak only to themselves
tremulous hands reach out
for turkey plates
covered with the cold gravy
of countless years
they scatter in the dining room
old forsaken quail
nesting alone
at cold white tables
fumbling with memories
and spoons

Thanksgiving 1978

Elegy in a Barbershop

I remember my childhood barber,
hair slicked back with tonic—
a chubby man in a bow tie,
sleeves rolled to the elbows,
thick hands smelling
of Vitalis and talcum powder.

He'd chat with retirees
who came to read his paper,
drink his coffee, and complain.
Restless, I brushed away
the thick brown curls
that piled up in my lap.

Now he's much younger.
We are alone in a small booth
without an audience.
I struggle to stay awake.
He clips and asks (as always)
about my golf game,

the cutting time much shorter.
His shears whisper elegies
to boyhood days in barber chairs
and to all forgotten smells—
thin gray hair falls
into my fingers. I fondle it.

Always keep old memories and have young dreams.
— Arsene Houssaye

Her Rings

To Mom

Her rings keep falling off,
even if she secures them with string.
She is losing herself,
her keys, pocketbook, rings.
All around her the afternoon
fidgets about its business.
The only sounds—the shuffling steps
of the old, straying down
the last halls of their days.
They wait unsettled in dusky rooms
to lie in the cool clutch of evening.
Outside the air hangs over the hill.
Herons nestle in tall pines.
Everywhere, a lingering smell
of last things.
She sleeps, wrapped
in the husk of the past.
Tomorrow, and days after,
she will phone at sundown to ask
if I have her rings.

You Still Speak to Cicero

Mother dear, you were a fine Latin teacher.
I can see you now, reciting Virgil
and Caesar before those adoring classes.
Fifty years passed in an eye-blink
before you were losing your car in parking lots.

The doctor spoke of plaques and amyloid—
some rogue gene that brought slow devastation
to your brain. Now a void of neurons hangs
like an old moth-eaten sweater, where once
a solid weave of bold thought reigned.

Yet you clung to the sacred virtues of Latin.
After you had forgotten most of our names
you still spoke on occasion to Cicero.
Tonight your spirit hunts for clues as it wanders
among the mind's gray convolutions.

Now and then it finds a Rosetta stone of memory—
an old Crosby tune and your eyes dance,
a smile wrinkles an empty face.
As I watch you now I see cells and neurons wink out
one by one like the lights of a sleepy village.

Manor Nursing Home
November 1996

To My Other Self

Our mother did not die easily.
She lived to almost ninety-six,
surviving "assisted living"
until hip fracture took her down.
Those years of visitations,
"mini-strokes," incontinence,
and demented phone calls
ended on a gray September day,
two weeks shy of her birthday.

She seemed to sense, to rally
when you were at her bedside,
and smiled for us only then.
You were her favorite, quiet one.
That day you held her hand
for hours while whatever "self"
was left there of herself,
inside of herself, fluttered
like a moth in search of an exit.

Shooting the Doves

In the forties my father worked two jobs.
A veteran of the Great War,
he planted a flag pole
in our front yard after Pearl Harbor.
On those twelve hour workdays
I only saw him at suppertime.
Then, with no warning, he left us.
The county ambulance hauled him away,
and he did not come back.

He was breaking a promise—
his promise to take me hunting.
I was to learn how to lead a dove,
how to aim for its next move into emptiness.
He had often told me
a boy must learn to shoot a gun
because someday he might be called to war.
We were to walk together in the dove fields,
blowing frost behind the dogs.

Uniontown
May 3, 1945

When Thanksgiving is Over

It's not turkey and cranberries we will miss—
not the eighteenth-century dining room table
decorated in paisley and a fall harvest
or the rare taste of homemade rolls—
not the Dallas Cowboys on TV
or afternoon naps after too much wine.

It's the silence around the table
when grandfather called us together
to ask the Lord's blessing.
It's dove shoots in pastures
after a noonday stuffing and baby brothers
eating custard from our spoon
as they twist and fret in highchairs.

It's touch football in the back yard
and running in stride with uncles and fathers
while shadows spread at first dark
and doves mingle and call
from the still green limbs of cedars.

We miss things most we never had.

Homecoming

He pledged Kappa Sigma in 1914
and savored a few college years
before he joined the army,
crossed the Meuse, and fell
in the Argonne forest.

Back home in a Hoboken hospital,
the thrill of homecoming
had no chance against the smell
of poison gas and death.

Long after he died,
some of his mail tracked me down,
his namesake, and Kappa Sigma
marked him living
when the mail did not return.

I maintained his living
with a gift to the alumni fund,
and in the computer he grew older.
Someday they will come to see him,
their oldest living member.
I will have to answer the door
and go to his first homecoming.

On a Bus to Maine

I wrote my name in frost
on a window pane
like blackboard days in school
with crumbling chalk
and haunting childhood dreams.
With letters stroked
by my fingers,
the cold glass pane took my name,
then melted it into the night.

Now I wish for classrooms
and well-spelled words
on old blackboards
like our parents used.
I want to write names
with chalk again
with letters that will not fade.
I want to stand
at the board and feel
white chalk on my hands.

Revised from original in
In the Country of Rain

On a Late Afternoon Drive

On a late afternoon drive
I return to my boyhood home
and the rounded rocks of childhood.
They have worn well.
A single day stands still
among the thousands of a long life.
Oaks have lost their leaves
after fall's chemotherapy.
Doves putter about in gray fields.
Sidewalks are empty.

I drive past a creeping town bus.
An old man in the bus window
 is wearing the face of my father—
so identical that I drive
beside the bus block after block
backing up traffic.
It is a moment of nearness
to an old man who is not my father,
but who is still alive.

When Summer Yields to Fall

A new hint of coolness in early morning air,
fading green leaves atop the sycamores,
the first streaks of cirrus clouds replacing
the cumulus cotton-wool clouds of summer—

It would be so different if any of these
were missing is the feeling you always have
on the first day of autumn, no, the first day
you think of autumn, when somehow

the outside tables of sidewalk cafes begin
to fill up in evening and a subtle awareness
of an earlier sunset are the signs of Summer
telling you that here is where he stops

and will no longer be walking with you.
Ahead a faint chill rides the evening breeze.
On a distant street corner stands Fall,
an amber shawl draped around her shoulders.

Revised from original in
As Fate Would Have It

New Poems

A poem is a place where the conditions of beyondness and withinnesss are made palpable, where to imagine is to feel what it is like to be. It allows us to have a life we are denied because we are too busy living.

— Mark Strand

Middle C

As a boy, I wanted to play the piano.
In my tiny town there were no teachers,
the nearest thirty miles away.
Wilbur, my classmate, could play Chopin
even though he was an insufferable nerd.

Then when I was over eighty years old,
watching Beethoven's Piano Concerto No. 4
convinced me it was time to learn to play.
Armed with a keyboard, I began lessons.
Just another goal to conquer, I mused.

Patiently, I played with one hand, "The Bear,"
"Clowns," and "Little White Pony," counting
and singing the simple childhood words.
Although my fingers were short and thick,
I was often reminded I was a good typist.

Then on my computer I watched Horowitz
play Chopin's Polonaise in A flat major,
his fingers, more ancient than mine,
dancing effortlessly over the keys.
I knew then I would never play Beethoven
and should be content to master Middle C.

Young Love

One of us loved more than the other
and often at different times
but we were young and far apart.
There were many things
we'd never faced nor understood.

Even when we were together
we could not always know for sure
what the other person felt.
It seemed that one of us would forget
those new and tender thoughts

the other remembered so easily.
So young it finally became apparent
that life ahead was too complicated—
that each day would bring
a new and different taste to the table.

Uniontown
circa 1949

A Broken Mirror

Memory is the sense of loss,

and loss pulls us after it.

Late in our days memory shatters

like a broken mirror

into jagged edges, nothing

you'd want to touch.

Holes open without images,

a home we once knew gone dark,

faces of grandparents forgotten.

The dead are speechless

while we sweep up pieces

and search for meaning

in shards of broken glass.

Winter Solstice

Outside this window, clear and cold,
a pale and shallow graying sun
awaits the planet's tilt to winter
and the shortest light of day.

As the moon rises above the hill,
a sly wind gathers forces,
and trees, in their black silhouettes,
link their winter arms.

December 21, 2015

A Prodigal Son

The past beats inside me
like a second heart.
Childhood loneliness
that brought life
to my imagination left me
as I grew up, looking
for a new place to belong.

I am a prodigal son
who returns to his home
to relive the freedom
of live oaks, whippoorwills,
and butterflies in summer.

Through them a moment
of peace: their voices—
the moan of a dove,
the owl's evening haunt—
all remind me tonight
that the challenge of solitude
is measured out equally
for everyone.

Poem Speaks for a Mortal World

Poem, we have known each other so many years.
In my childhood you taught me the importance
of words, words to drive away sadness of heart.
You had me memorize Tennyson and Milton
and attempt to write imitations of famous poets.

You taught me to rhyme and to sense meter needed
to make my poems become walls against loneliness.
When I chose medicine my childhood self died
but came back years later when I sought words
to ease the pain of dying for the bereaved.

After that you were close by as I wrote poetry
about so many things my adult self said and felt.
Now the words don't—or won't—come anymore.
I wonder if they were ever mine?
Tell me...my adult self, the poet, is dying, isn't he?

But then, *Poem*, you say immortality for me
could be intolerable, eternal life even unbearable.
In death you believe there is no self to suffer,
no need to worry anymore as all our memories
of sadness or failure are erased like words on a page.

What We Do Not Hear

Wind and rain, birds and clouds—
they all have something to say
and speak to us every day—

as to why the wind should skip
from bamboo hedge to elm and oak
making leaves talk but not to each other—

as to why sunlight slips in random
through branches of winter-sleeping trees
to bring light and speak to anyone there—

or as to why crows circle overhead,
cawing in voices we do not understand.
Even low cumulus clouds travel

with voices that yearn to speak to us
of distant lands and silent caravans.
There is so much more to hear than

the mourning dove down in the cedars,
rain pelting magnolia leaves,
or the wind in old elms at first dark.
So much more—if we listen.

*Whatever its actual content and overt interest, every poem
is rooted in imaginative awe.*
— W. H. Auden

In the Solitude of Sleep

While darkness covers a sleeping world,
before the doves call and first light
slips in beneath the curtains,
he feels the hoof beats of centuries
thundering outside his window.
They run hard—white stallions in single file—
to reach him before light steals in
and strips away cloud covers, fading moons,
to bring him voices as he sleeps.
Voices speak of endless caravans and lands
but remain silent to those who leave
the land of sleep and gather on city streets
or the banks of slow-moving rivers
where no one lives or breathes alone.

Advent 2015

how short the days are
how slowly the traffic moves
down overly decorated streets
past the old faces of houses
revived with Christmas lights
and wreaths as winter solstice
returns under gray skies

choruses of "Jingle Bells"
drown out the hymns of Advent
as children search the sky
for red-nosed reindeer
instead of an infant child
and grownups are content with
a partridge in a pear tree

pride has replaced humility
and infected many of us
in another Yuletide epidemic
as we come bearing gifts
for family and friends and see
how revered the Christmas tree
how short the days

December 21, 2015

Their Secret

They conceived us,
our mothers and fathers,
they gave us names.

When we were infants,
they clothed and fed us.
When we grew up,

they picked our schools,
our churches,
even childhood friends.

Then they cut us loose
to find our way,
make our own decisions,

to watch them grow old
and demented, then die,
taking with them

the secret of where
we came from,
from what wet sea.

Senior Reflections

Kindness can deceive us
if we crave it like an addict
or shame us if we have to remember
what we haven't done or been.

At every chance that comes along
I like for things to go my way
but please don't confuse
what I just confessed with honesty.

There are so many kinds of loneliness
yet only that one vague word
for those who lie awake with no one
except the light in the bathroom.

Happiness is a state of mind
one should never enter
into with any hope of staying long
on a road that doesn't exist..

I've known the emptiness
of being in a room someplace
with nothing at all to say to anyone
and lived contentedly with it.

Solitude shuts out the world
we must endure and those friends
whose platitudes remind us
to be grateful for being alone.

Secret Love

The widow Maude and Major Alexander have rooms

at Paschall's boarding house on Spring Street.

She knits and listens to her radio

while he plays chess or smokes his pipe alone.

No one there knows that she knits him a scarf

or that the Major pays her rent each month.

Dirty Bottoms

How do we know it's spring?
We often ask
when Mother Nature plays
her games to fool
both us and the azaleas
that sleep in late winter.

But clouds may tell of
its arrival as they drift
in their layers above.
Those clean cirrus streaks
high in the sky
or mid-altitude gray balls
of stratocumulus clouds
do *not* herald spring.

Watch and wait, instead,
for slow-moving clouds
carrying rain that darkens,
their lowest layers—
rain to nourish early azaleas
and blooming peach trees—
watch for low-hanging clouds
with dirty bottoms.

Morning Paper

Coffee and the morning paper
often start the day for the retired,

the front page predictable
after nightly TV news.

But then, the obituaries—
those little sums of infinity,

those lives crammed together,
with date of arrival and departure,

blurry photos of the young, then old,
the beginning and the end—

condense all our living
and our dying onto a single page.

It's Time

Weekdays can be boring in retirement—
on Thursdays I push the trash bin to the curb
where the newspapers are waiting
to see if I will read the sports and ignore
the carnage of the world, the obits, the DUIs.
I should be glad I'm not in morning traffic
going to the same workplace another year.
Instead I drink coffee and delete dull emails.

But this Thursday is different—fall is here.
The wind sounds different in the trees.
A good time for a brisk walk, I ponder,
but settle back in the porch swing
and think about trying to write poems again.

Yellow leaves are gathering in the yard;
the birds are gone, summer feels over,
yet somehow I remember it is the equinox—
a day in a year three-quarters gone when
the sun appears equal to the coming night.

All around me the day and the dark descend
as fall waves to me from the front yard.
Her chill wind reminds me it's time
to put on sweaters and rake the leaves—
time to sit back and feel the breeze.

Thursday, September 22, 2016
Autumnal Equinox

Sounds That Bind Us

There are sounds that speak
to the randomness of our being—

the homeless wind speaks to us
as do the waves of the sea,

cedars groan when doves call
at first dark, wordless melodies

drift among flower beds.
These sounds bind us,

hold us together
until the Earth no longer sings.

Survival Instinct

Life's basic pleasures remain unchanged,

       as do its minor satisfactions—

planting a garden, building a fire,

       watching pelicans glide

in formation before they dive for mullet.

       Survival instinct we call it

as we try not to think about sadness—

       of which there's never a lack—

and walk on, wiser, cleansed,

       for having imagined this,

holding on to the world as we know it,

       somehow keeping it alive

and vibrant should tomorrow arrive.

Pensacola
circa 2014

To Be Alive on Shore

There comes a time
when time is not enough,

when it is time to be alive
by a lake where the sun dies

in the evening,
leaving a sky so empty

that it has no end.
Glintless, the sun sleeps

in the lake where all creek beds
pour their nothings,

where a shadow on the water,
soft as thought, slows,

waves gently, as if
some shadowy life with which

it might be one, be none,
beckons to anyone alive on shore.

To Be A Sea Snail

This evening someone has been speaking
to me in a strange way. I have been sad,
and everything looks dark around me.

Nothing will change, the voice spoke to me.
*You will go on although you live in a shell
in your smallness, like a sea snail.*

But because you struggle, I will wait for you,
the voice said, *and time will wait
for you to evolve, my friend—you will survive*

*the mouth of the sea bass and the gull's beak.
When you finally arrive, it will be as if inside
the live oak not a single ring has grown.*

*It will then be your time to leave the shell
of smallness and bring light into your life,
to sink roots and to grow like the live oak.*

*What imagination is—it is only the lie we must learn to
live by, if ever we mean to live at all.*
— Robert Penn Warren

Heartstrings

Fifty years of long corridors
to waiting rooms with welded chairs,
bearing news that held each family
like needle, thread, a knot.

Simple explanations were allowed—
a clot, a tear—but assurance was made
that everything was done,
yet the body held its own weak will,
its faulty pump a failure.

A wife who's been otherworldly still,
listens for a word, a gentle pull
on a chain that softens the harsh cry.
For her, the heart must have soft strings.

Their Morning Guest

In antiseptic, windowless rooms
I am their morning guest
after wandering so many nights
among the almost dead.

So as not to feel too close
I touch with gloved hands,
palpate what wilts beneath skin.
They do not want me to read

prayers or gospels from holy books.
If someone asks to see results
of all the blood tests, x-rays,
and scans, I will reveal to them

what was hiding in their veins,
show them ghosts captured on film,
bodies in slow surrender.
That's all they want from me.

Our False Centrality

If this is a timeless world
in which we live,
life should not be linear,
not locked
into the past and present.
We are not central
to anything
if time is endless.
Time needs no center.
This gives us room
to imagine everything
that is or has been
or will be.

February 29, 2016

*Imagination is more important
than genius.*
— Albert Einstein

Cold Winter Mornings

On some cold winter mornings
I still remember a poem by Robert Hayden,
a black poet, entitled "Those Winter Sundays"
written in the tumultuous sixties
when his people again sought emancipation.

His father, who labored during the week,
would also arise early and make fires
to warm his family on Sunday mornings.
The poet recalled no one ever thanked him
and sensed the chronic anger of his father.

I remember cold winter mornings
when Richard, our black handy man, came
quietly into our bedrooms, laid and lighted
fires of kindling and coal, walking softly
while humming a cheerful tune.

We leisurely dressed in warmth for school,
had breakfast, and waited for our carpool.
He went about each day doing his chores
with pride and always an honest smile.
We never thanked Richard either.

Uniontown
circa 1945

85

The Untreatable Body

An old medical school professor
who taught anatomy told my class
something like this about the body:

No matter which one you get,
you will never be satisfied.
Wherever you go, day after day,

you will carry it with you.
As it ages, you have to bear
the unfaithfulness of skin and bones

for which the few changes
you can make are small and costly.
Someday you will follow

what you have seen others do
who were much like you,
and who, on occasion without

warning, left behind their lump
of skin and bones to remind
everyone of life's imperfections.

My Addiction

Tonight I had my monthly injection.
It flowed through my veins
and focused my failing eyes

after a month of waiting.
Now I can breathe deeper again
for a while, even smile at strangers.

It brings back old favorite songs
of the forties and fifties I thought
long buried with friends I've lost.

It took me tonight by surprise,
crouched behind low-hanging clouds
in the east of Bayou Texar

when it rose—enormous, broad,
and dusky orange in the twilight.
Later, as I sat in my porch swing

I watched it climb between clouds
and age into a full white moon,
a ghostly galleon on a winter cruise.

Pensacola
January 2016

This Life

For Barbara Crafton

It is a mystery for those
who travel it on a linear path
but not for those living
outside a limit of time
who may know what we do not.

While we ponder the afterlife
versus the alsolife and wonder
if there are those outside
our realm who know the answers,
there is a blessing we ignore.

It is life itself, something
as common and finite as it
is precious and inexhaustible,
something that endures
and surpasses all understanding.

Poets and Poetry

How do poets compare to poetry?
A good poem has eternal life.
It holds itself together in one piece
but eventually we, the poets, do not.
To those ungifted writers,
 it is always elusive, to be envied,
the thing hardly anyone can do.

Over the years our ears
become deaf to poetry's rhythm,
hidden in the language all around us.
We do not sense its iambic pulse,
those memorable bits,
those metaphorical transformations.
We do not let it enter our dreams.

Once we welcomed those words
that came in dreams just before dawn.
We even jotted them down on a notepad.
Now as we grow old, our days shorten
yet we still cling to bits and pieces,
favorites that have one thing in common:
memories of a life we soon must lose.

To Become a Poet

When I am asked how I began writing poems
I speak about the indifference of nature.
It was the day of my father's burial,
a chilly May afternoon with a cloudless sky.
No breeze stirred the limp leaves of trees.
I sat on my grandmother's porch swing,
looking at day lilies and roses in the garden
that seemed oblivious to my sadness.

There was no cheerful chorus of bird song—
only the distant cawing of crows.
The air was still and solemn about me—
the only smell was the sweet scent
of funeral flowers in the front parlor.
I sat all alone on that porch swing
and placed my grief in the mouth of language,
the only thing that would grieve with me.

Father's Day
June 20, 2015

Things

Lucretius wrote poetry about things
when poetry made more sense
than winged angels and demons.
To him all human beings were made
of the same stuff as everything else
and part of the natural order.

Lucretius lived before Christ and sensed
the emptiness of pagan gods. He believed
everything was made of particles.
Time was unlimited, space unbounded.
There was no afterlife. The soul died
with the body. Religions were delusions.

Belief in afterlife and a divine creator
came later, yet some still feel a mortal world
is enough, not an easy goal but possible.
Not knowing what awaits us in that cottage
of darkness, we should keep this world alive
with the light of living all around us.

If we are all particles, let us respect birds
and trees—all life on land and sea—
the voices of clouds and wind in trees,
sunlight filtering through the elms
on late winter afternoons, and surely
each other. Lucretius would be pleased.

On the Nature of Things
— Lucretius

His Christmas Wish

After four score and four,
his gift is a preview
of what was inside
the cottage of darkness.
When he returns,
in the light, he brings
a message for everyone,
his days numbered.

It is near time to go.
Things are wearing down.
The cardboard Santa Claus
that had stood beside the tree
since he was five or so
can only be propped up
by the wall, its colors
faded and almost gone.

The family, too old or tired
for Christmas Eve Mass,
can only attend the childrens'
service in the afternoon.
Piles of presents under the tree
leave paper and ribbons
that are picked up before
other presents are opened.

(2)

Children no longer believe
Santa can come down
all the world's chimneys
the night before Christmas.
They do not seek oranges
in their stockings but reach
instead for expensive gifts
that should be under the tree.

It's time to start all over
and bring some innocent faces
together again under the tree—
to put aside canes, walkers,
and skip afternoon naps—
to play and sing favorite carols,
and go to Midnight Mass—
time to be children again.

Christmas 2016

Grandmother's Porch

For years it seemed
her porch would sing
with a voice
like the cracking of bone

under the weight
of them all—
uncles, aunts, cousins.
Slowly, one by one,

they were plucked away
like lint from a worn sweater.
Left there together,
grandmother, an old friend,

the dog, sat listening
to the sobbing of leaves
after fall had swept through
the windblown trees.

Fall 2016

Derek

"Sir, what's your name?"
the policeman asked me as he stopped his cruiser
beside me while I was taking my daily walk.
"Looking for a man about your age named Derek.
He's been missing since early this morning.
He's wearing blue jeans and a blue shirt," he added,
staring at my khaki pants and white T-shirt .
"Call 911 if you see him," he then advised
as he pulled away. Within five minutes he returned,
slowing down to say they had found him.

Tell me, Derek, did you just want to get away
and be alone? Or were you looking for something
new outside your living room and TV?
Perhaps you were even searching for the road
you walked as a boy carrying your fishing pole?
Derek, I have to wonder if you've done this before.
You must still be healthy if you're able to walk alone.
Now that you are found, will they put you away
in some dismal nursing home you despise,
or will they give you another chance, my friend?

The Widower

At night she keeps him ghostly company,
she or someone who speaks
from the bedroom corner in her voice.

He realizes he must pick up constantly
as the departed did. Her memories, too,
require her favorite food and drink.

He moves carefully from room to room
to avoid her good-natured rebukes.
She had a way of saying to him

that something as simple as opening
a bag or a can could've been handled
with a little more grace.

My Debate with Nature

I sought out Nature in my back yard
one evening to debate the scheme of things
designed versus the many faces of Nature
it said had no bad intentions or motivation.

Nature bragged about glorious sunsets,
moonlight and lilies of the valley,
misty mornings, a star-studded sky,
even the strange beauty of swamps.

In contrast it scoffed at me—
at our weapons of mass destruction
created by man to destroy man,
our cleverly chosen words that disguise

and justify greed and lust for power.
Not to be outwitted, I reminded Nature
of its natural non-motive crimes—
earthquakes, tornados, hurricanes

that demolish schools and stores,
trailer courts, even homes for the elderly.
I topped off the debate by bragging
of spaceships and heart transplants.

I made it clear that I prefer artificial
man-made things, the skill involved,
without which we'd have no insight,
no accurate view of who we are.

Your Winter Walk

As you put on winter clothes
and walk under gray skies,
tell yourself that you will go on,
listening to the drumbeat
of your heart wherever you are.

If you should grow weary
during your walk in the cold,
you may lie down at nightfall
and rest beside the road
under the warmth of winter stars.

One day, when you realize
you cannot go on or turn back,
remember to tell yourself,
when cold begins to fill your body,
that you love who you are.

Title Index

TITLE INDEX

All of Henry Langhorne's books, except for *Tombigbee*, *Listen to the River*, and *Winter Clothes*, are available at amazon.com.

In Search of Solitude is also available online from Barnes & Noble and other major outlets.

All of the books, except for *Listen to the River*, which is out of print, are also available from the publisher.

Pelican Press Pensacola
P.O. Box 15131
Pensacola, FL 32514-0131
850-206-4608
pelican.post@att.net
www.pelicanpresspensacola.com

About the Author

Henry Langhorne, former Poet Laureate of Northwest Florida (1999-2009), is the author of ten collections of poetry: *Tombigbee* (1999), *Listen to the River* (2001), *Winter Clothes* (2003), *The Clarity of Last Things* (2005), *As Fate Would Have It* (2007), *In the Country of Rain* (2009), *The Lay of the Land* (2011), *The Canebrake Collection* (2013), *In Search of Solitude* (2015), and *Light is Life* (2017).

For over twenty years, his poems have been published in a number of local and regional periodicals, including: *The Sewanee Review (Winter 2016)*, *Hurricane Review*, *The Panhandler*, *Emerald Coast Review*, *Poem*, *Negative Capability*, *The Cape Rock*, *The Chattahoochee Review*, *Plainsongs*, *Passager*, *Inlet*, *Mediphors*, *Life on the Line* (anthology), *Dockside*, *On Wings of Spirit* (anthology), *The Pharos*, and the *Journal of the American Medical Association* (JAMA). He is currently a member of the Academy of American Poets.

Henry Langhorne graduated from The University of the South at Sewanee in 1953 and then attended Tulane Medical School. His internship and residency were at Charity Hospital in New Orleans and his cardiology fellowship with the Tulane Department of Cardiology. In 2016, he received his MFA in Creative Writing at Sewanee, becoming the oldest graduate to receive a degree there. He retired in December of 2014 as the senior member of Cardiology Consultants, after practicing cardiology in Pensacola, Florida, since 1962.

Made in the USA
Coppell, TX
28 August 2021